Magical Pet Vet

The Yeti Who Coughed Up Confetti

By Jason M. Burns
Illustrated by Renata García
Colors by Larh Ilustrador

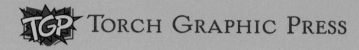

Published in the United States of America by Cherry Lake Publishing Group

Ann Arbor, Michigan

www.cherrylakepublishing.com

Reading Adviser: Beth Walker Gambro, MS, Ed., Reading Consultant, Yorkville, IL

Book Designer: Jason M. Burns

Torch Graphic Press is an imprint of Cherry Lake Publishing Group.

Library of Congress Cataloging-in-Publication Data has been filed and is available at catalog.loc.gov

Cherry Lake Publishing Group would like to acknowledge the work of the Partnership for 21st Century Learning, a Network of Battelle for Kids.

Please visit http://www.battelleforkids.org/networks/p21 for more information.

Printed in the United States of America

Corporate Graphics

Note from publisher: Websites change regularly, and their future contents are outside of our control. Supervise children when conducting any recommended online searches for extended learning opportunities.

TABLE OF CONTENTS

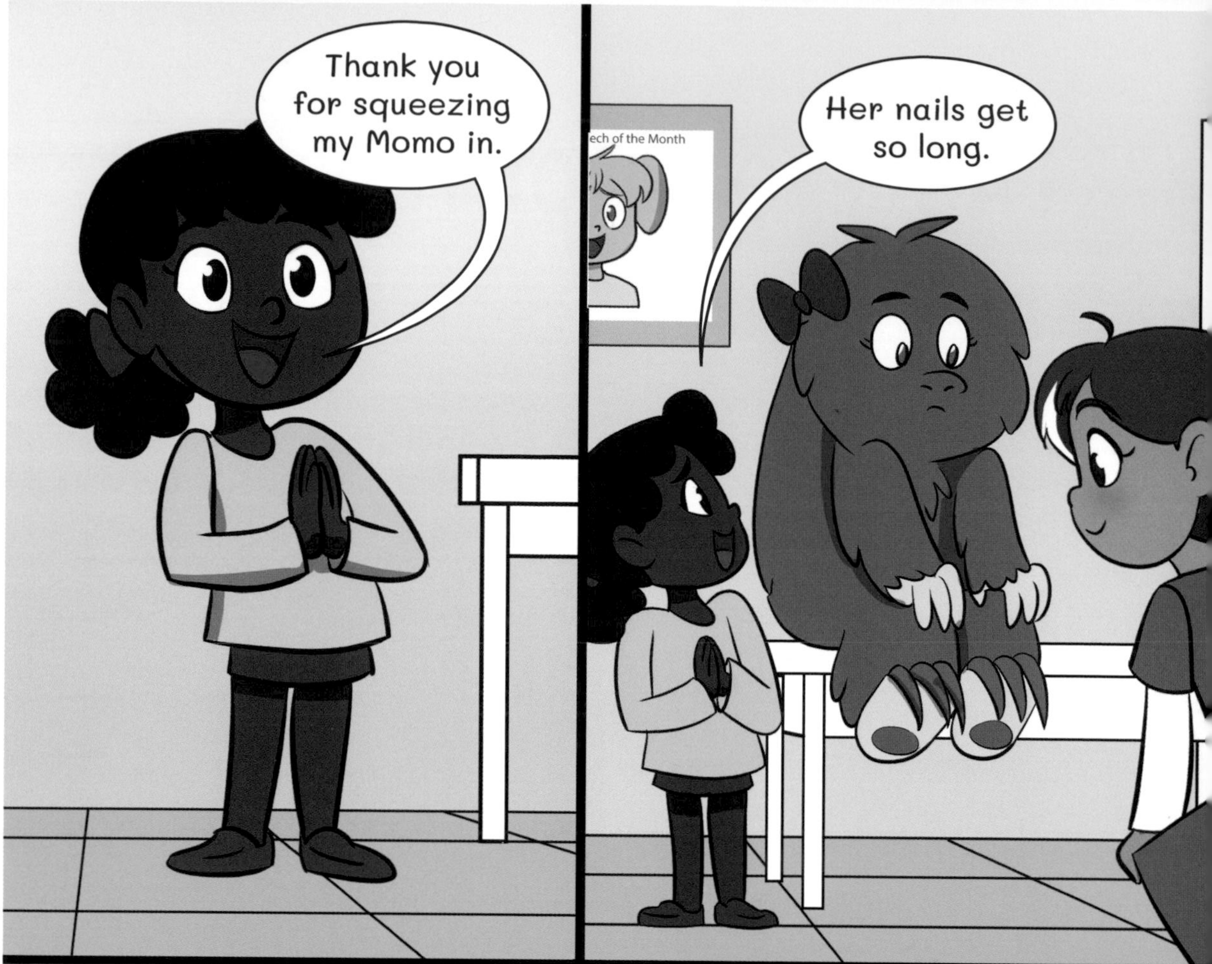

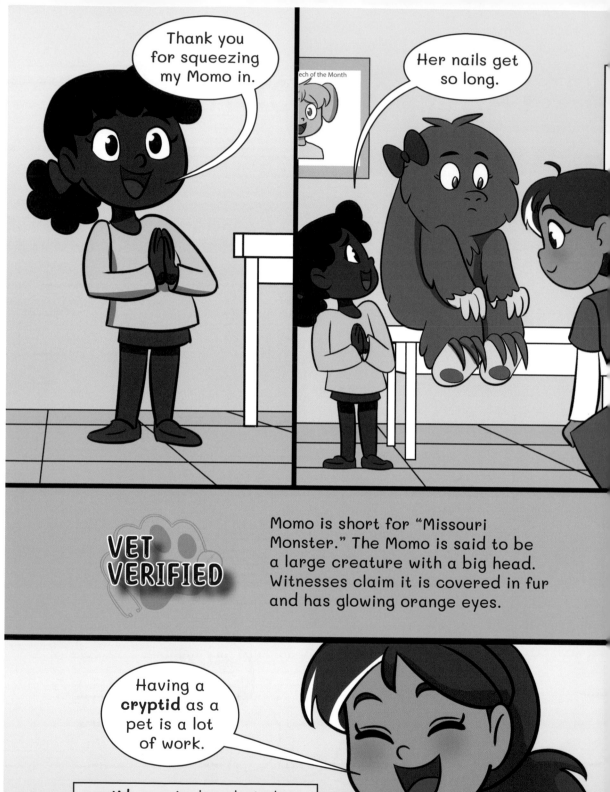

Thank you for squeezing my Momo in.
Her nails get so long.

VET VERIFIED

Momo is short for "Missouri Monster." The Momo is said to be a large creature with a big head. Witnesses claim it is covered in fur and has glowing orange eyes.

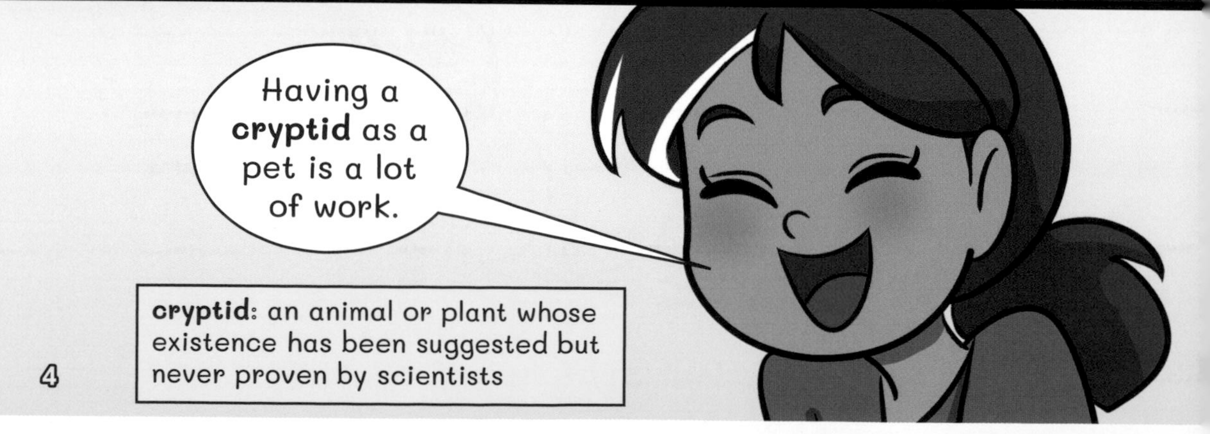

Having a **cryptid** as a pet is a lot of work.

cryptid: an animal or plant whose existence has been suggested but never proven by scientists

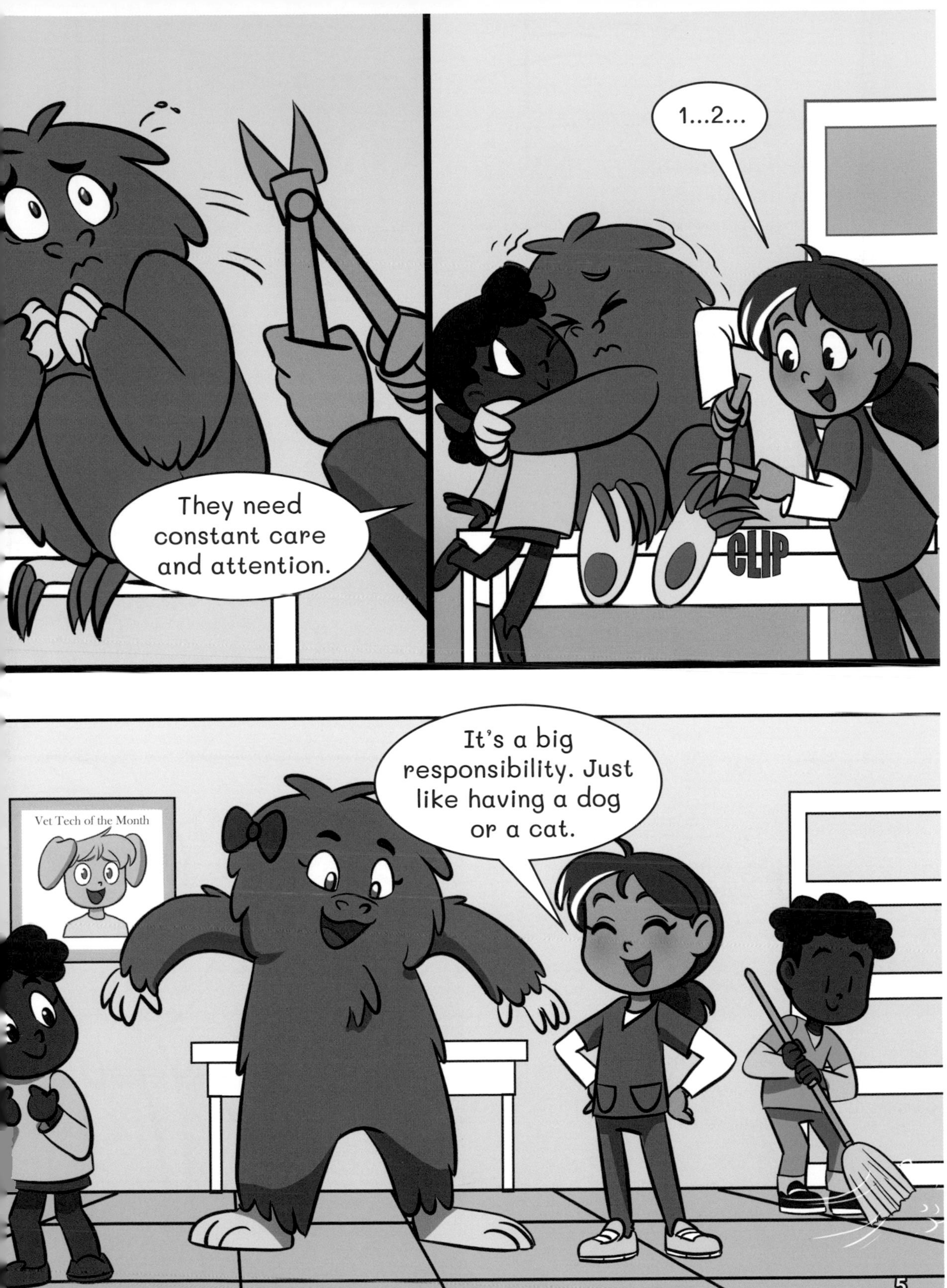
They need constant care and attention.
1...2...
CLIP
Vet Tech of the Month
It's a big responsibility. Just like having a dog or a cat.

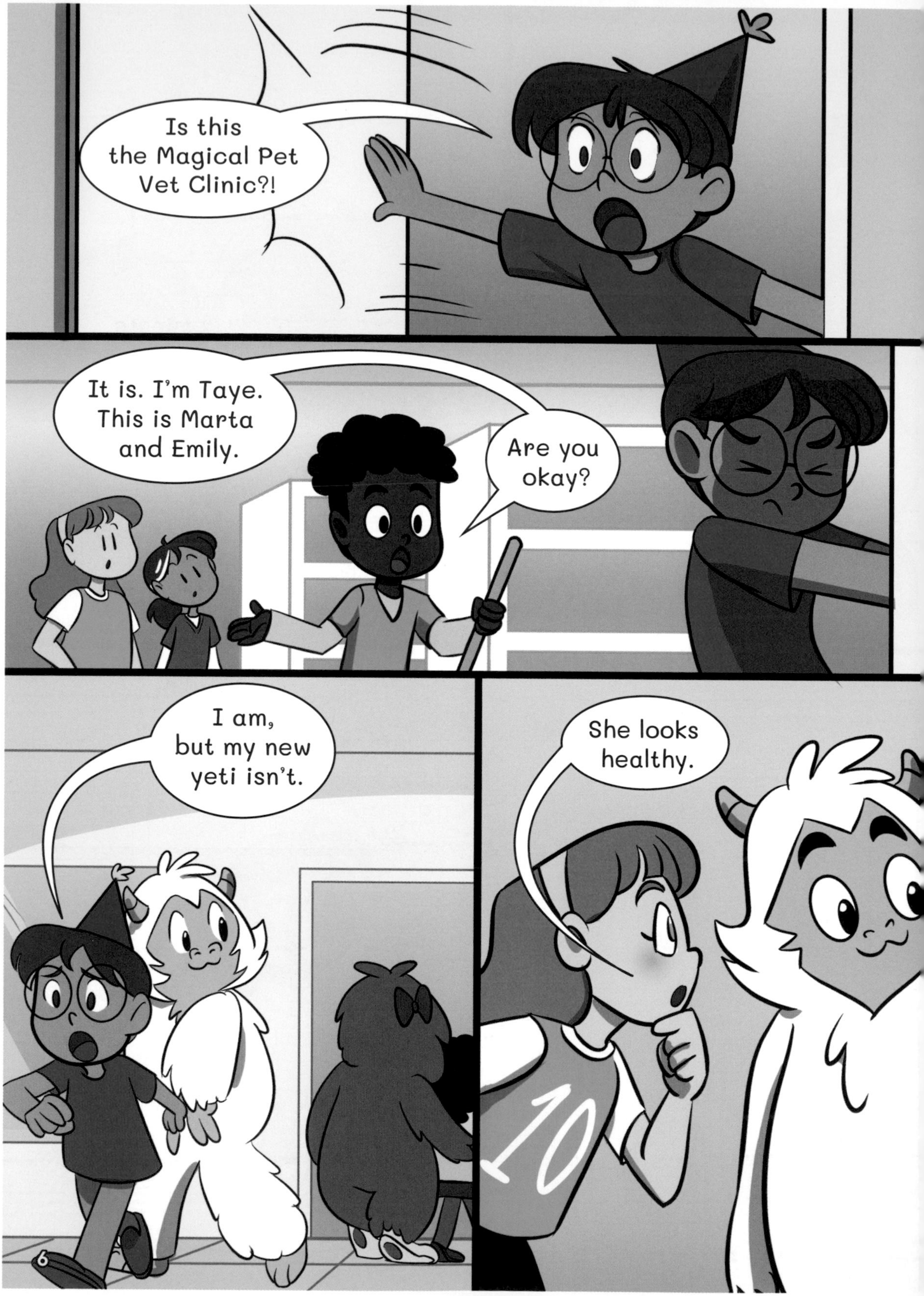
Is this the Magical Pet Vet Clinic?!
It is. I'm Taye. This is Marta and Emily.
Are you okay?
I am, but my new yeti isn't.
She looks healthy.
10

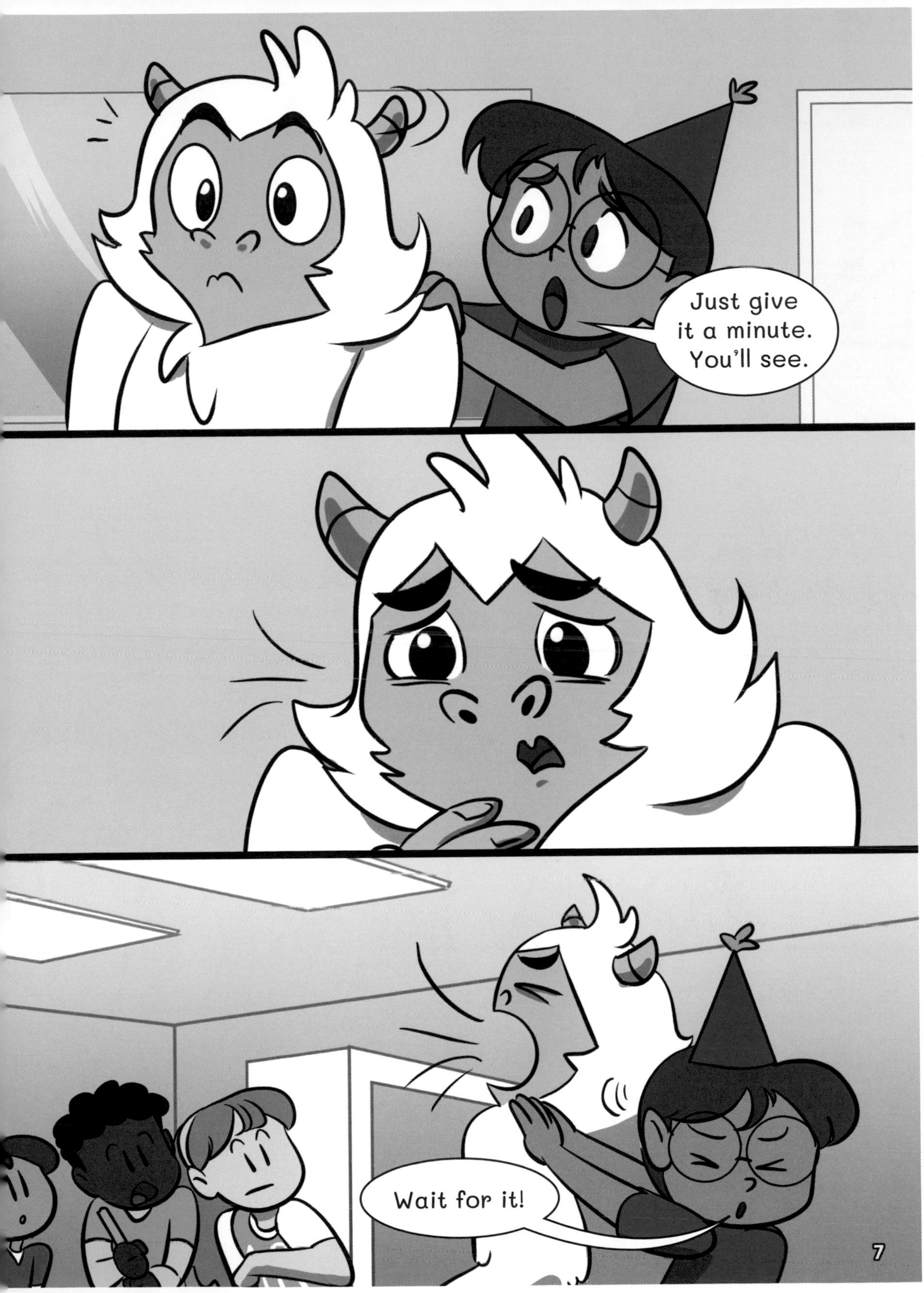
Just give it a minute. You'll see.
Wait for it!

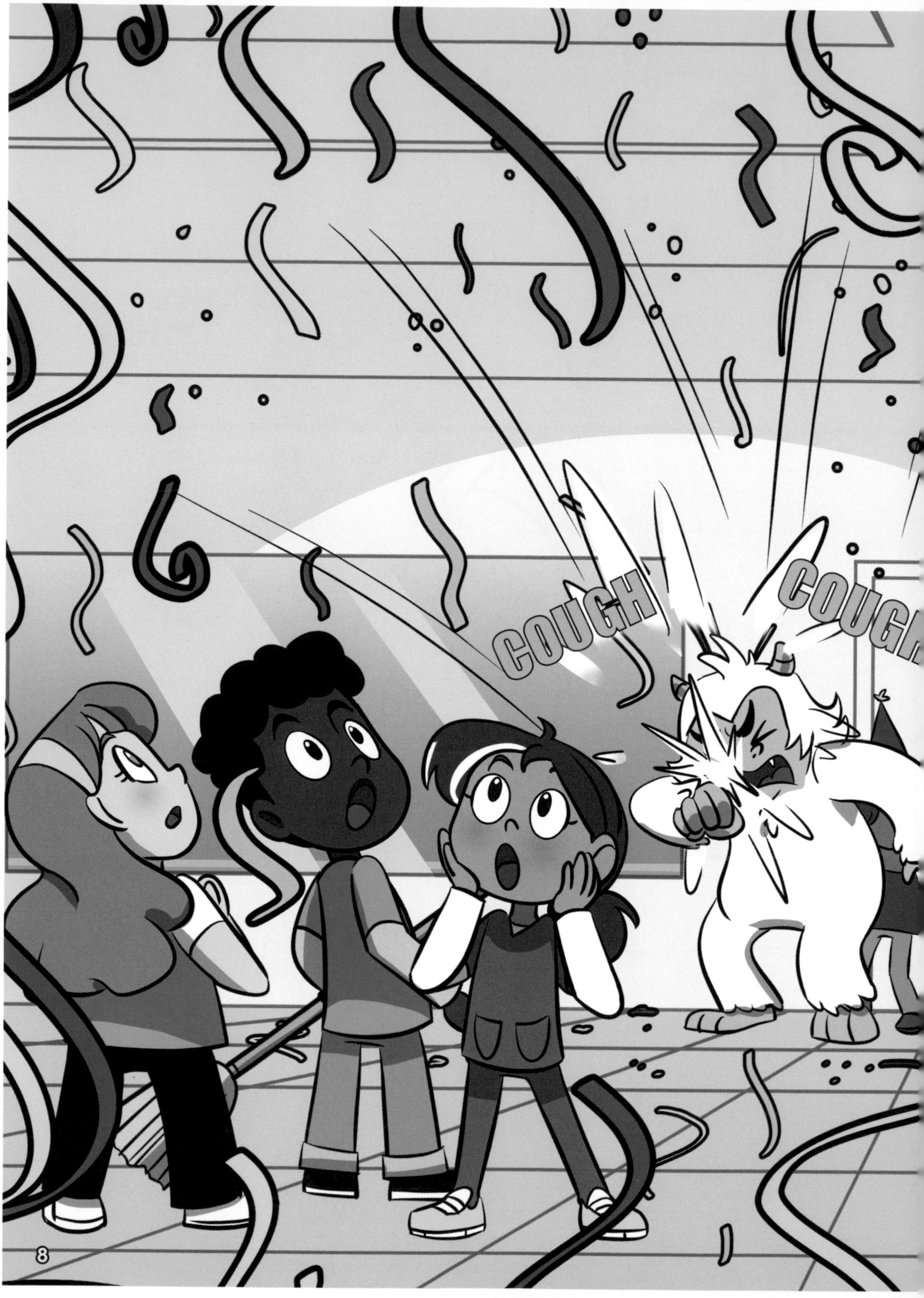
COUGH
COUGH

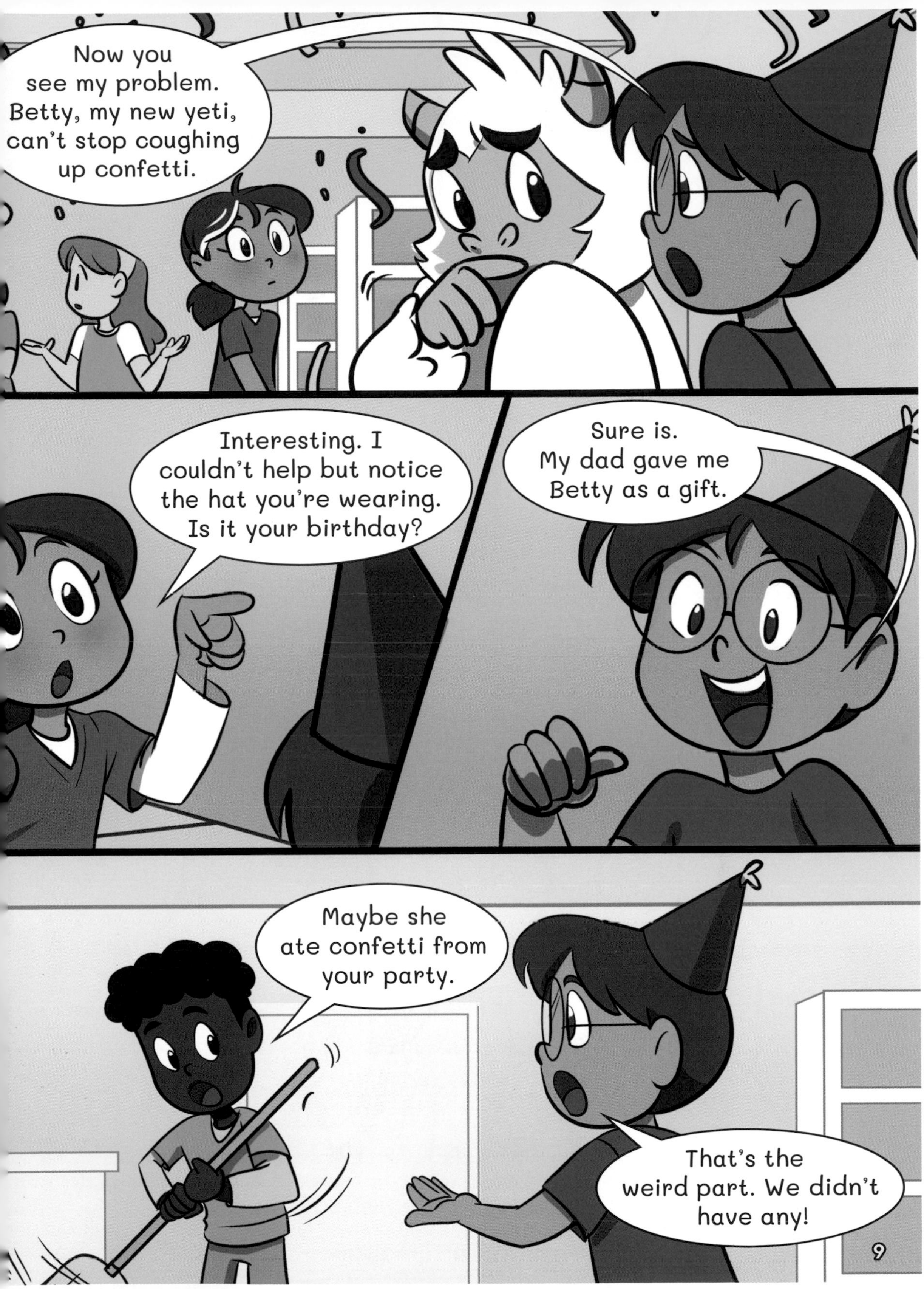
Now you see my problem. Betty, my new yeti, can't stop coughing up confetti.
Interesting. I couldn't help but notice the hat you're wearing. Is it your birthday?
Sure is. My dad gave me Betty as a gift.
Maybe she ate confetti from your party.
That's the weird part. We didn't have any!

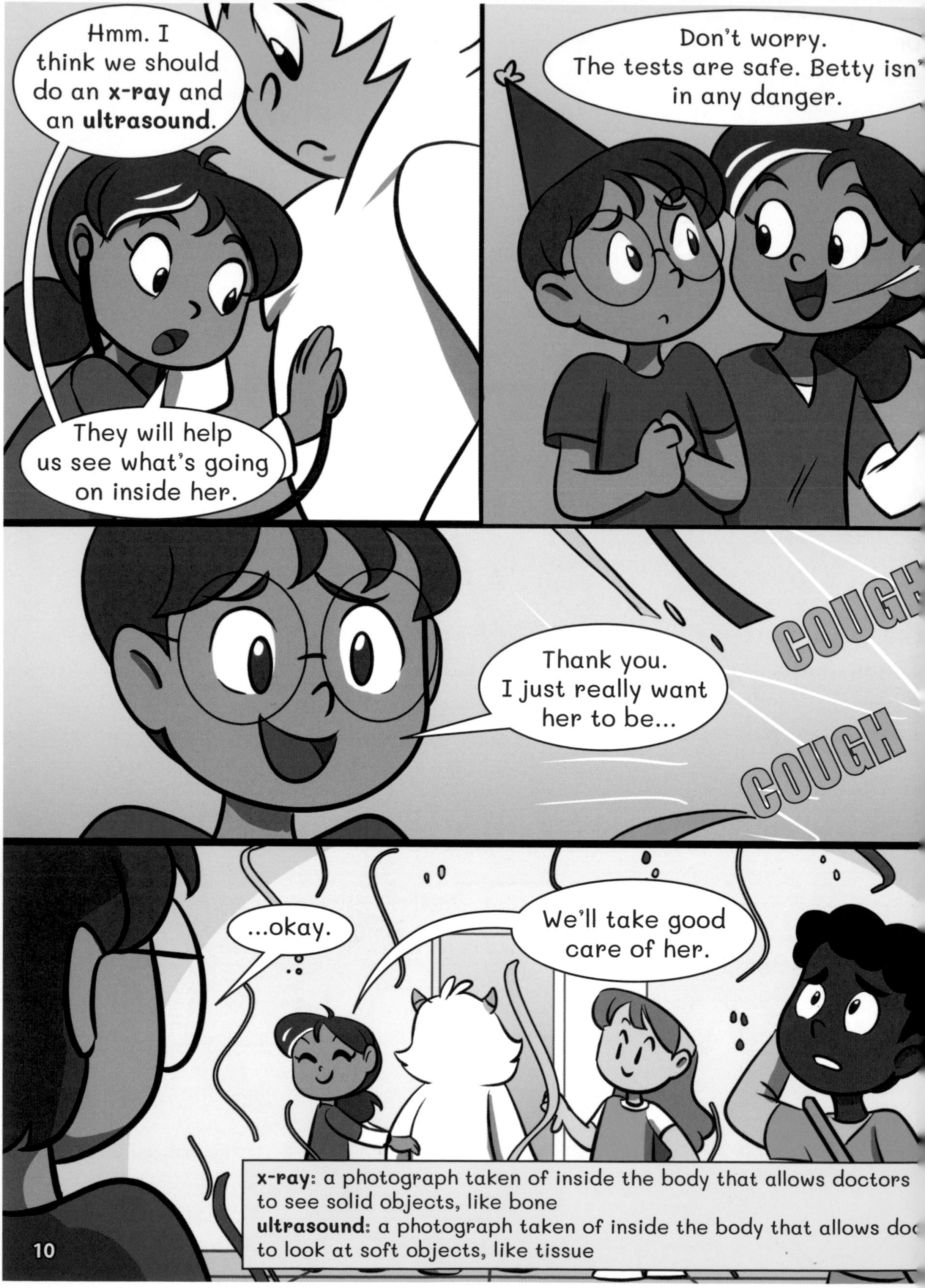
Hmm. I think we should do an **x-ray** and an **ultrasound**.
They will help us see what's going on inside her.
Don't worry. The tests are safe. Betty isn'
in any danger.
Thank you. I just really want her to be...
COUGH
COUGH
...okay.
We'll take good care of her.

x-ray: a photograph taken of inside the body that allows doctors to see solid objects, like bone
ultrasound: a photograph taken of inside the body that allows doc
to look at soft objects, like tissue

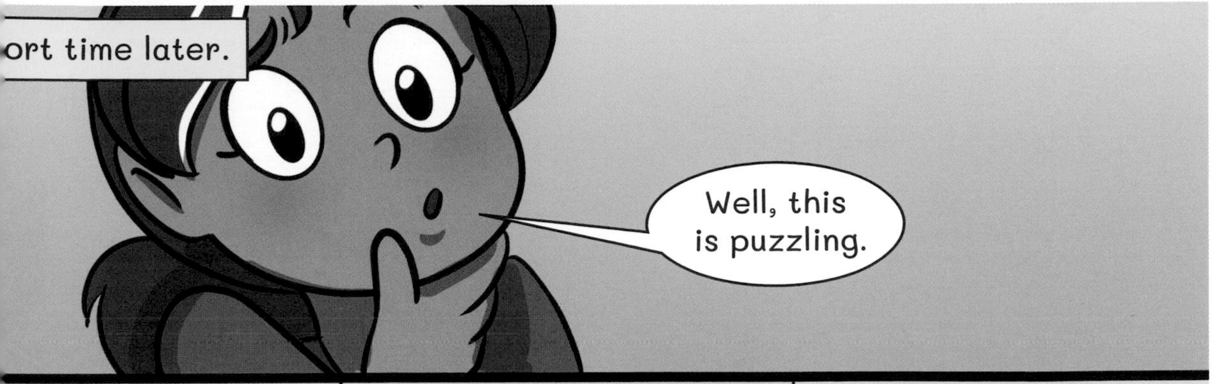
ort time later.
Well, this is puzzling.

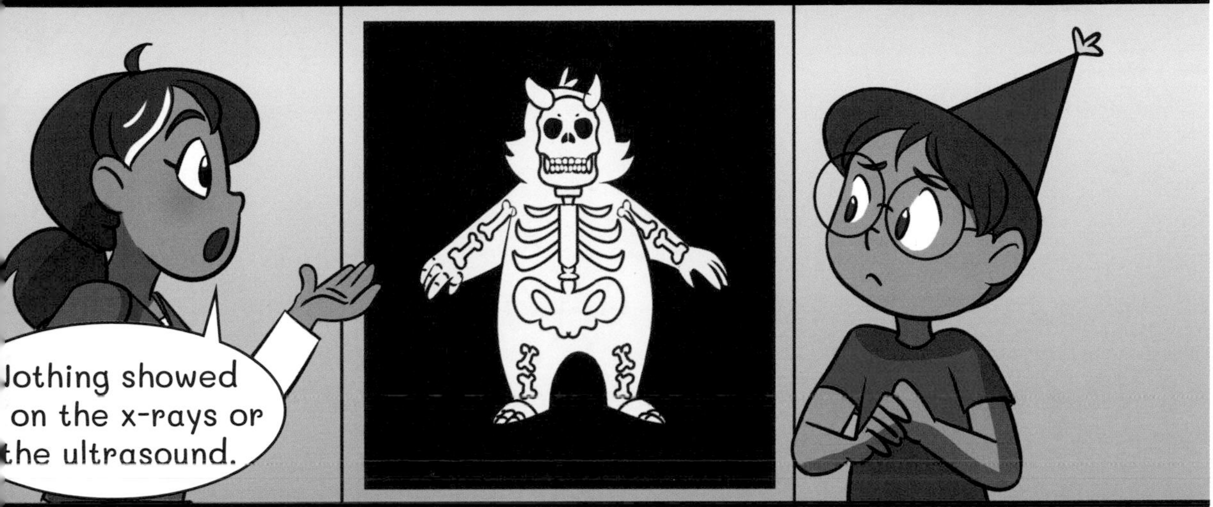
othing showed on the x-rays or the ultrasound.

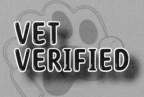

VET VERIFIED

Veterinarians are trained to give animals x-rays and ultrasounds. These tests help locate broken bones and find diseases like cancer. Dogs and cats also eat things that they shouldn't. Objects like toys, string, and even socks inside a dog's or cat's stomach show up on x-rays.

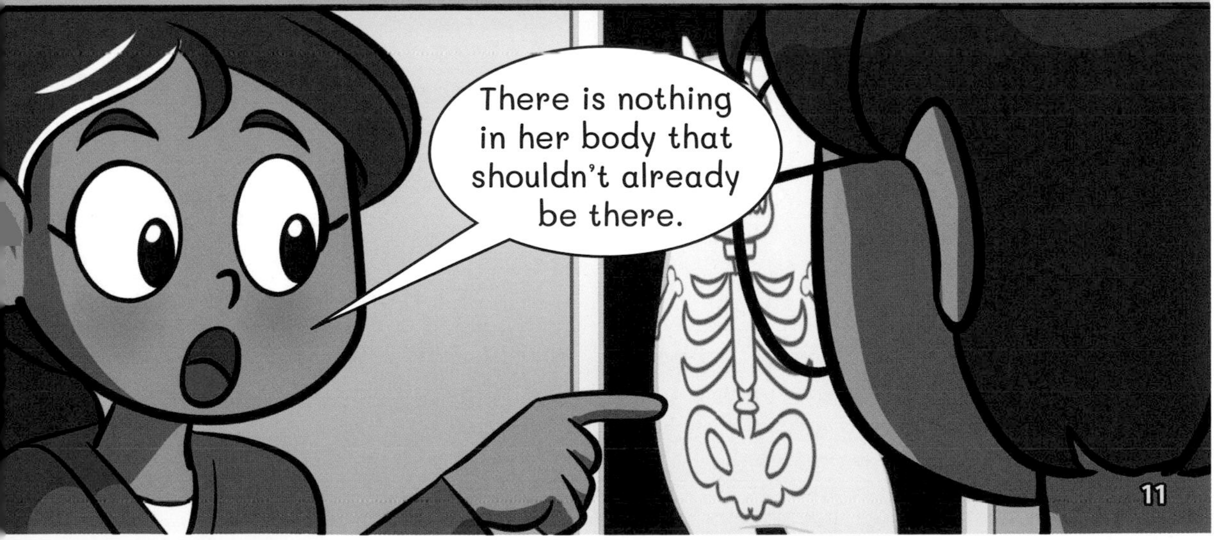
There is nothing in her body that shouldn't already be there.

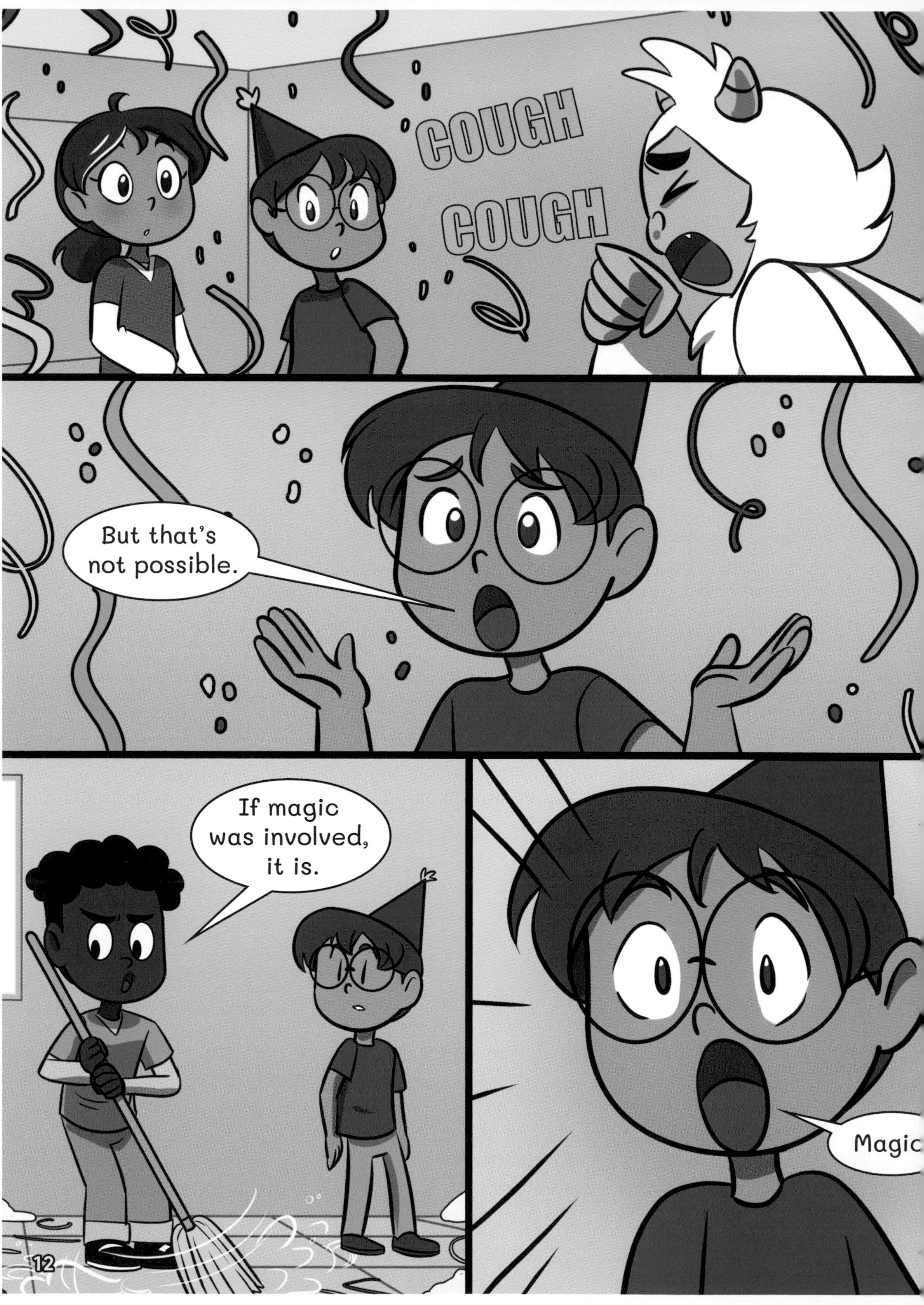
COUGH
COUGH
But that's not possible.
If magic was involved, it is.
Magic

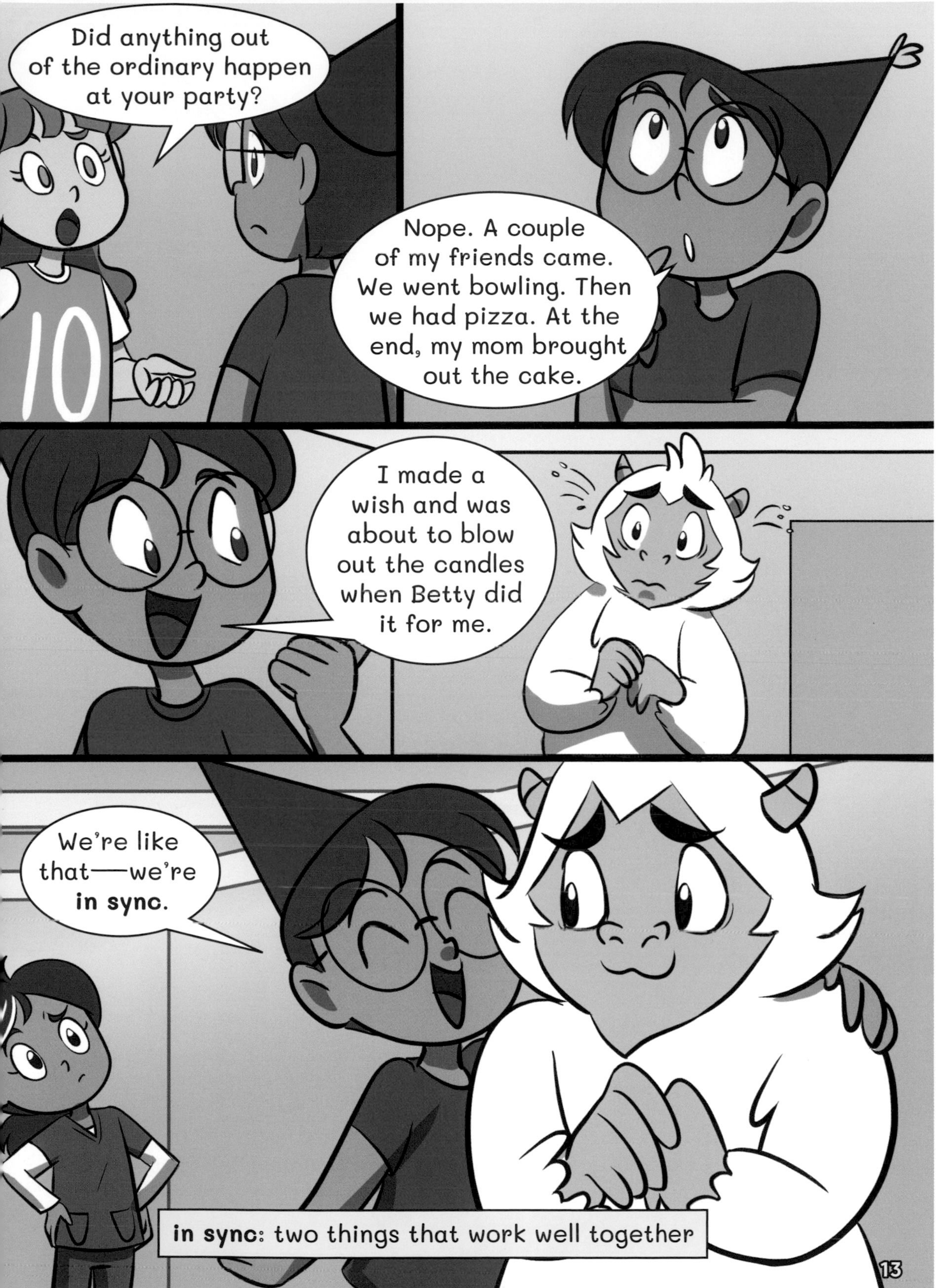
Did anything out of the ordinary happen at your party?
Nope. A couple of my friends came. We went bowling. Then we had pizza. At the end, my mom brought out the cake.
I made a wish and was about to blow out the candles when Betty did it for me.
We're like that—we're **in sync**.
in sync: two things that work well together

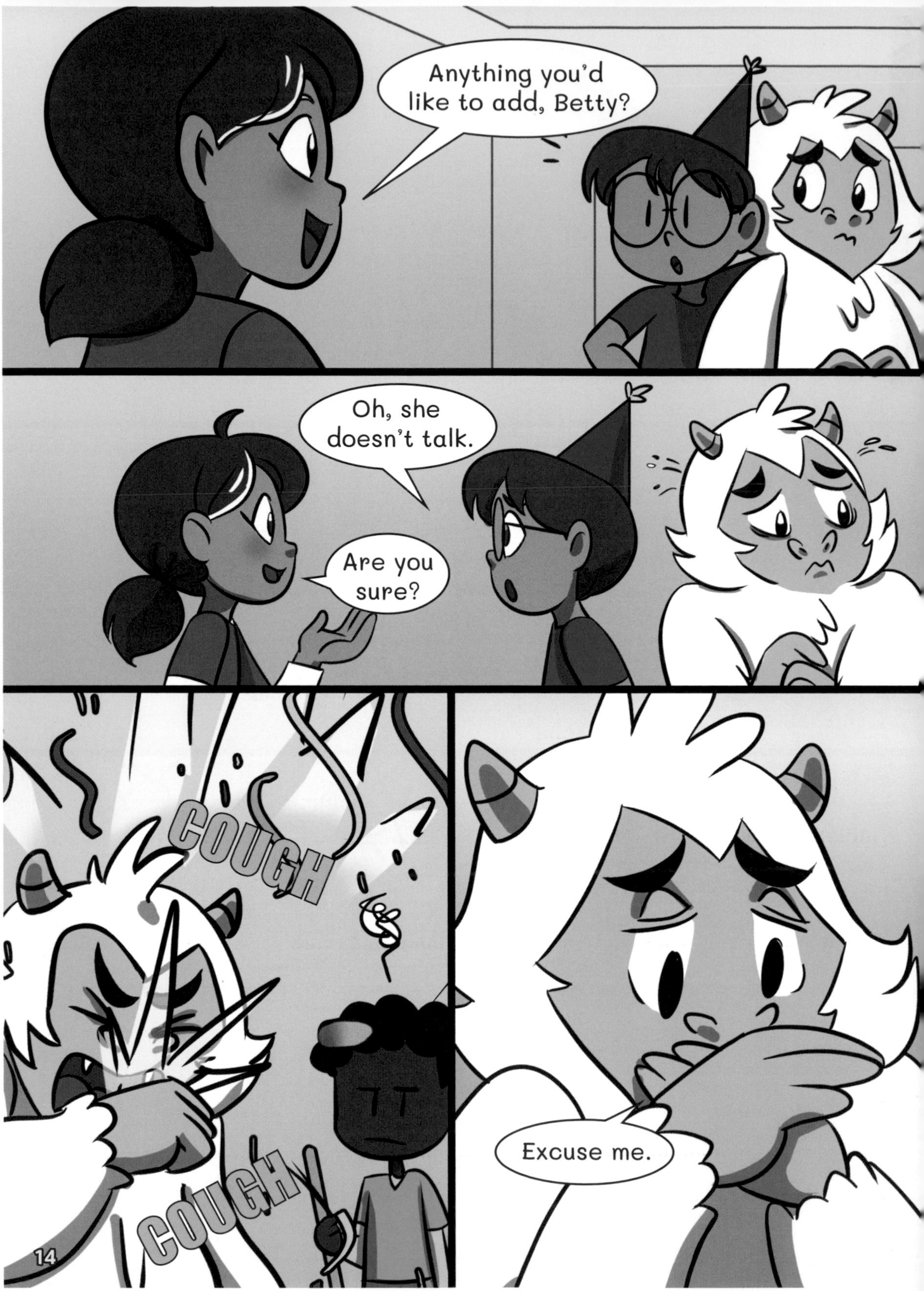
Anything you'd like to add, Betty?
Oh, she doesn't talk.
Are you sure?
COUGH
COUGH
Excuse me.

I'm sorry. I stayed quiet because I didn't want to scare you.

You *do* talk?!

The last family I lived with sent me back to the shelter when they learned I could talk.

VET VERIFIED

Many veterinarians recommend adopting animals from a shelter. You will be giving an animal in need a loving home.

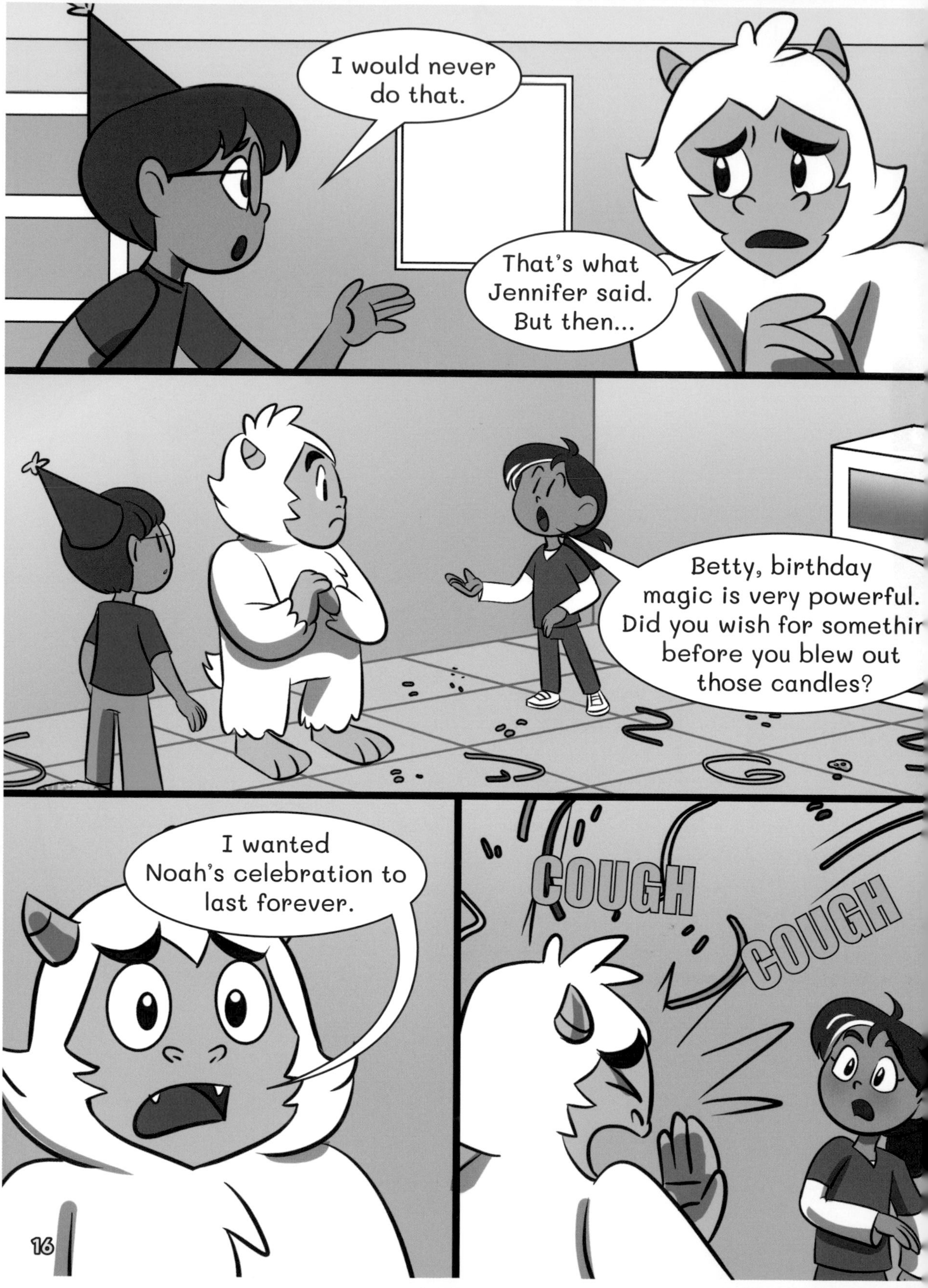
I would never do that.
That's what Jennifer said. But then...
Betty, birthday magic is very powerful. Did you wish for somethin before you blew out those candles?
I wanted Noah's celebration to last forever.
COUGH
COUGH

I thought that Noah's family would be less likely to send me away if Noah was happy all the time.

Your yeti, Betty, is coughing up confetti because she was feeling unsteady.

Emotionally unsteady, I mean.

UNLEASHING UNDERSTANDING

There are many reasons why someone would act differently than they normally would. A lack of **confidence** is one of them. People who are uncomfortable with themselves will pretend to be somebody that they're not on the inside.

confidence: being sure of yourself

17

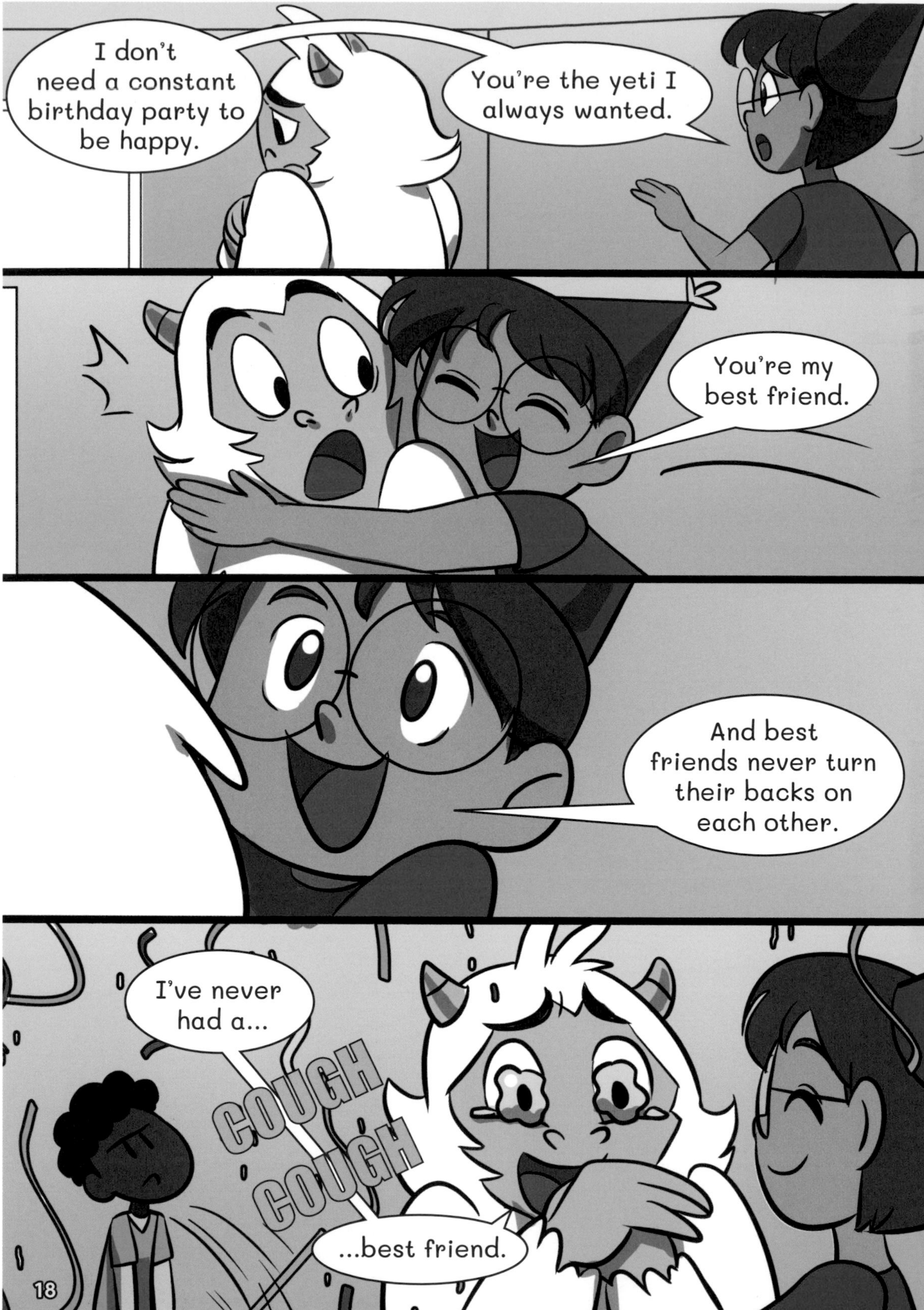
I don't need a constant birthday party to be happy.
You're the yeti I always wanted.
You're my best friend.
And best friends never turn their backs on each other.
I've never had a...
COUGH
COUGH
...best friend.

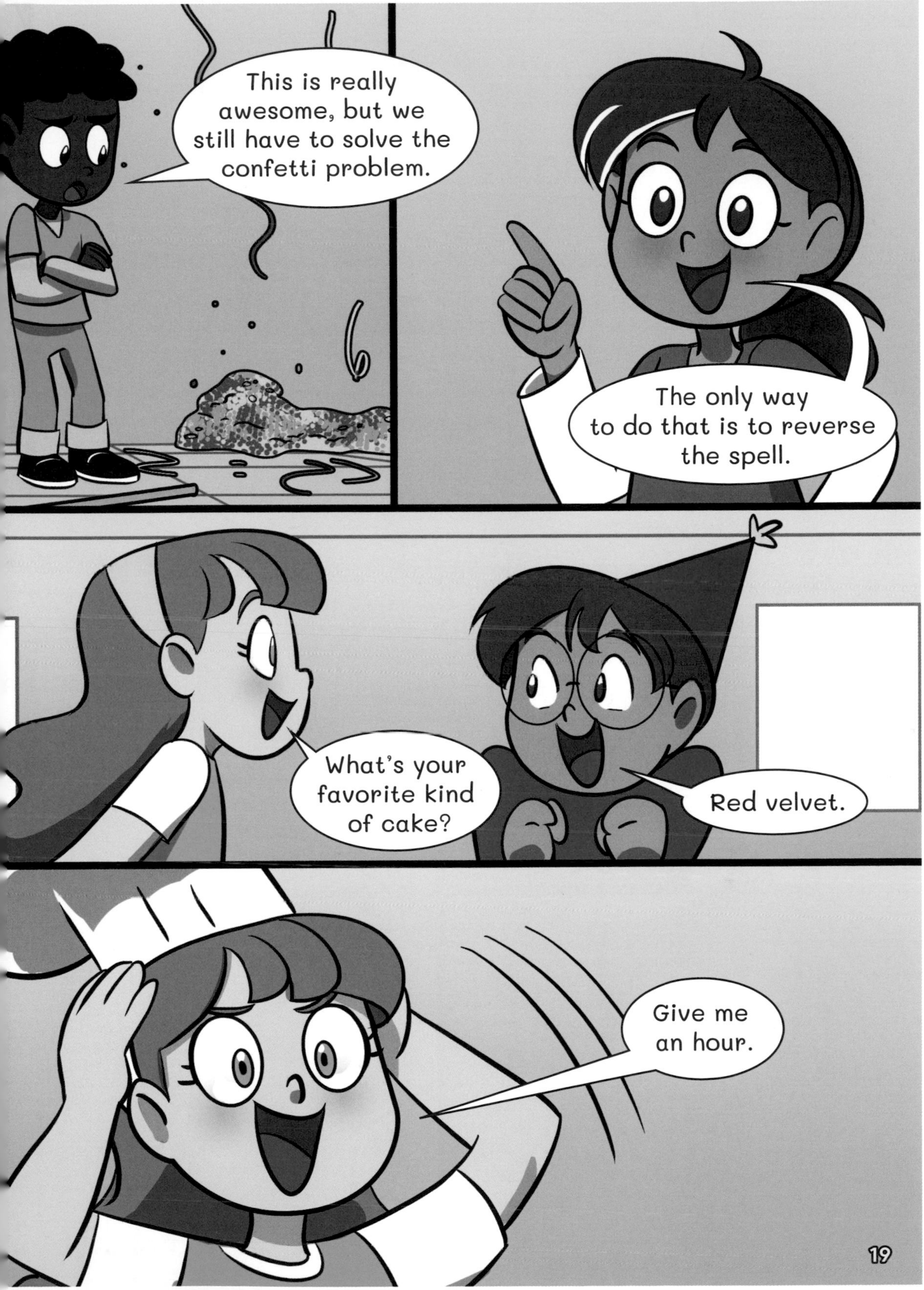
This is really awesome, but we still have to solve the confetti problem.
The only way to do that is to reverse the spell.
What's your favorite kind of cake?
Red velvet.
Give me an hour.

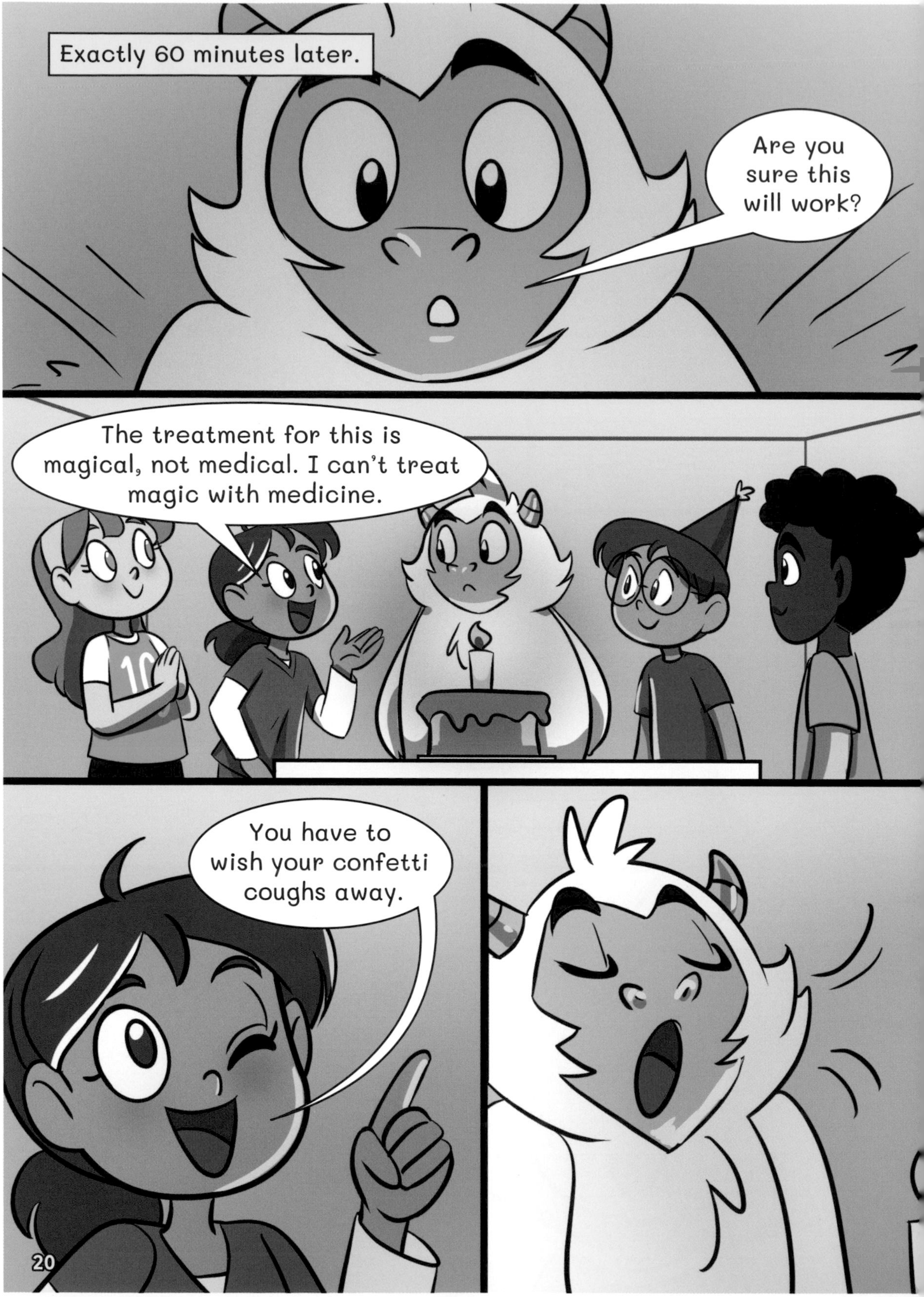
Exactly 60 minutes later.
Are you sure this will work?
The treatment for this is magical, not medical. I can't treat magic with medicine.
You have to wish your confetti coughs away.

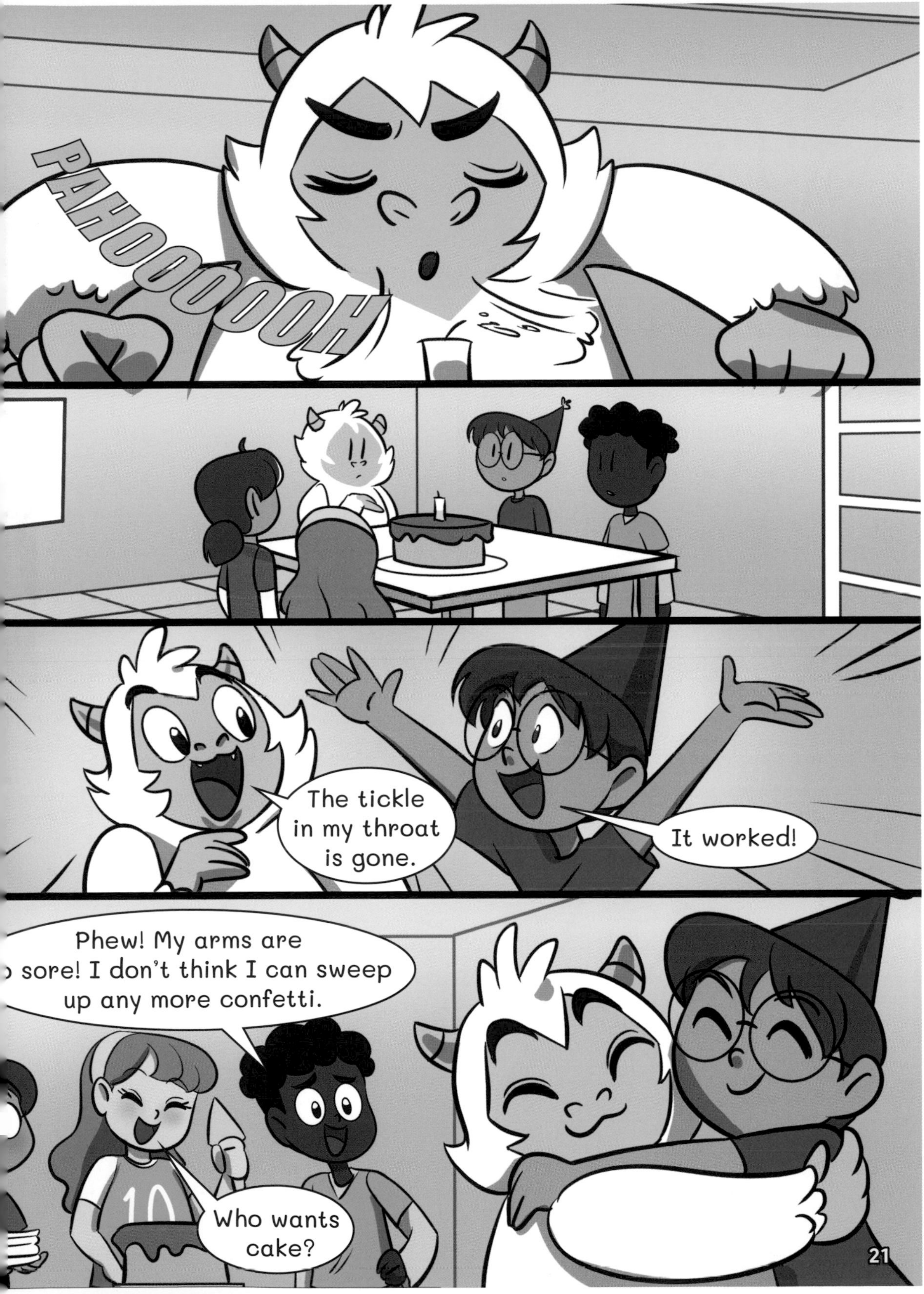
PAHOOOOOH
The tickle in my throat is gone.
It worked!
Phew! My arms are
sore! I don't think I can sweep up any more confetti.
Who wants cake?
10

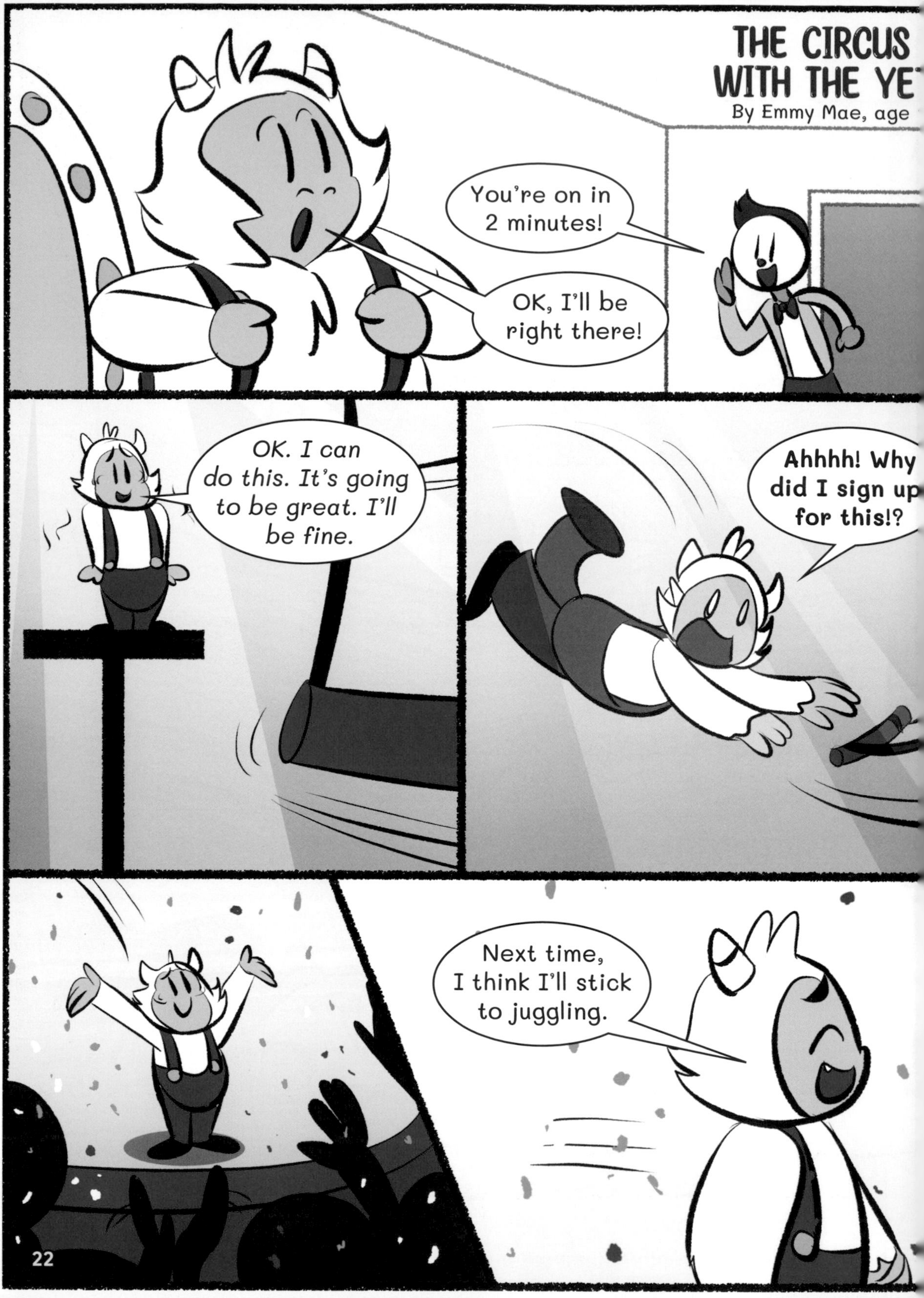
THE CIRCUS
WITH THE YE
By Emmy Mae, age
You're on in
2 minutes!
OK, I'll be
right there!
OK. I can
do this. It's going
to be great. I'll
be fine.
Ahhhh! Why
did I sign up
for this!?
Next time,
I think I'll stick
to juggling.

Learn More

BOOKS

Ha, Christine. *Yeti*. Mendota Heights, MN: Apex, 2021.

Troupe, Thomas Kingsley. *How to Find Bigfoot*. Mankato, MN: Black Rabbit Books, 2023.

EXPLORE THESE ONLINE RESOURCES WITH AN ADULT

The Conversation
Curious Kids: How Do X-rays See Inside You?
By Karen Finlay

Dogtime
15 X-rays of the Weirdest Things Ever Found in Dogs' Stomachs
By Mike Clark

Bios

Emily wants to become a professional football player someday. Until then, she is happy helping out at the Magical Pet Vet. Not only is Marta her best friend, but she has so much fun meeting all of the interesting creatures who come in for help.

Marta has always had a love for animals. Since she could dream she has wanted to be a veterinarian. When she discovered that there were creatures in her town that not everyone knew about—creatures many people think of as monsters—she opened up the Magical Pet Vet to help them stay healthy and happy.

Taye can create anything with technology. He has always understood machines. After becoming friends with Marta and Emily, he realized he could put his skills to use helping creatures in ways that even a doctor can't.

Glossary

confidence (KAHN-fuh-duns) being sure of yourself

cryptid (KRIP-tid) an animal or plant whose existence has been suggested but never proven by scientists

in sync (IN SINK) two things that work well together

ultrasound (UHL-truh-sownd) a photograph taken of inside the body that allows doctors to look at soft objects, like tissue

x-ray (EKS-ray) a photograph taken of inside the body that allows doctors to see solid objects, like bone

Index